National Museums Scotland

D0927241

The Clans

Gordon Jarvie

SCOTTIES SERIES EDITORS
Frances and Gordon Jarvie

Contents

Original edition published in 1995
by HMSO publications

Published from 2000 by
NMS Enterprises Limited – Publishing
a division of NMS Enterprises Limited
National Museums Scotland
Chambers Street, Edinburgh EH1 1JF

Revised and reformatted edition 2010
and 2019

Text © Gordon Jarvie 1995, 2000, 2010, 2019
Images (for ©, see below and page viii of the
Facts and activities section)

ISBN: 978-1-905267-44-6

British Library Cataloguing in Publication Data
A catalogue record of this book
is available from the British Library.

Book design concept by Redpath.
Cover design by Mark Blackadder.
Layout by NMS Enterprises Ltd – Publishing.
Printed and bound in the United Kingdom
by Henry Ling Ltd, Dorchester, Dorset.

CREDITS

*Thanks are due to the following individuals and
organisations who supplied images and pho-
tographs for this publication. Every attempt has
been made to contact copyrightholders to use the
material in this publication. If any image has been
inadvertently missed, please contact the publisher.*

COVER ILLUSTRATION
(© National Museums Scotland) – *William
Cumming, Piper to the Laird of Grant* by Richard
Waitt (1714)

NATIONAL MUSEUMS SCOTLAND
(© National Museums Scotland) – for pages 5, 7,
9, 11, 15, 17, 19, 21, 23, 25, 31, 33, 35, 37 (tartan
samples); 7 (Glenfinnan Monument, soldiers & Blair
Castle); 8 (Highland shepherd); 9 (targe, flintlock
pistol, dirks, sword); 10 Pictish harpist & Jarlshof
slate); 11 (broch); 14 (bow brooch & Finlaggan);
15 Eilean Donan Castle; 18 (Gaelic harp, piping
medal); 19 (chanter & *Piper to the Laird of Grant*;
20 (quaich & feast scene); 24 (Lowland wedding);
27 (Battle of Culloden & Highland Clearances);
29 (Kyle of Lochalsh, angler & soldier); 30 (kilt
wearing); 31 (sporrans, Highland woman);
32 (Falkirk tartan & dye stick); 33 (recruitment
poster [detail], Parisian fashion); 34 (Fiery cross);
37 (amber beads, rock crystal charm & clootie
well); 38 (Highland games & gathering posters);
39 (lumberjacks, emigrant ship & shinty stick).
Facts and activities section, page i (pipers)

FURTHER CREDITS (p. viii of Facts and activities
section)

SCOTTIE BOOKS

For a full listing of NMS Enterprises Limited –
Publishing titles and related merchandise:

www.nms.ac.uk/books

Some major Scottish clans

Anderson

Shetland Islands

Marwick

Sinclair

Mackay

Gunn

Ross

Morrison

MacLeod

MacAulay

Monro

Innes

Grant

Fraser

MacLeod

Leslie

MacDonald

MacKenzie

Macpherson

Forbes

Mackinnon

Gordon

MacDonnell

MacNeil

Cameron

Lindsay

MacDonald

Menzies

Robertson

Ogilvie

Maclain

Murray

MacLean

Drummond

Beaton

Graham

Campbell

Bruce

Macfie

Buchanan

Stewart

Livingstone

Seton

MacMillan

Ramsay

Montgomery

Home

Hay

Cunningham

Hamilton

Kerr

Scott

Boyd

Douglas

Elliot

Crawford

Johnston

Kennedy

Armstrong

MacDowall

Maxwell

2

Clan identity

MANU FORTI

GANG WARILY

BYD AND

Gordon – ivy

Drummond – holly

'With a strong hand'

Clan identity through the wearing of badges and plants was popular, especially during the 18th century. This was long before modern tartans became associated with the clans.
See pages 36-37 for clans associated with other mottos, badges and plants.

Mackay – bullrush

What is a clan?

A clan is a group of families, or a community of people.

Clan members usually have the same surname, and a chieftain who is head of the family. In the past, the chieftain relied on his clansmen to support him. In return, he gave them his protection. Clansfolk used to believe they were all descended from the same ancestor – sometimes a real 'historical' person and sometimes a legendary or mythical figure.

Clansfolk were often very loyal to their chief and felt themselves different to others who were not members of the clan. This is known as being 'clannish'.

Clann

The Gaelic word *clann* means children or kindred. It is possible to trace back – through history and legend – the family tree of many clan chiefs, sometimes over hundreds of years, to their traditional ancestor or **name-father**.

On the left is the family tree of Campbell of Glenorchy, which was drawn up in 1635. Sir Duncan Campbell of Lochow (or Lochawe), the founder of the Campbells of Glenorchy, sits proudly at the foot of his family tree.

The name-father

In the Middle Ages in Scotland, before people used surnames, they were known by their Christian name, plus 'son of'. For example, Iain MacEwen meant 'John son of Ewen'. This is known as the name-father.

The ancestor, or name-father, of the MacDonald clan was plain Donald. One of the great Gaelic leaders around 1200 was Aonghas Mac Domhnaill – that is Angus MacDonald. He became a great leader and chief of the clan. MacDonald became the family name, used by all of those who were descended from Donald. Clann Domhnaill – Clan MacDonald – means, therefore, 'the family of the son of Donald'.

The name-father of the MacNeils is Niall of the Nine Hostages, High King of Ireland in the fifth century. Other name-fathers were ancient pagan gods – MacFie or MacFee means 'son of the dark-haired fairy', while MacDiarmid means 'son of Diarmid', a hero of Celtic legend.

Lots of clansfolk were not related to their chief. They just took his surname as their own. So, if you lived in MacKenzie country you took that surname. If you moved over the hill among the Frasers, you took that surname. The chiefs encouraged this tradition in order to increase the size of their clans.

Tartan samples from a ledger collected by the Highland Society of London in the 19th century, sealed and approved by the donors.

Tartan check

The close association of tartan with name and clan is difficult to make before the nineteenth century, and there were no clan tartans around at the time of the Jacobite Rebellion of 1745. However, from as early as the 15th century, the word 'tartan' was used to describe quality cloth with colours woven in stripes and into rich checks. It was part of the decorative art of dress. Some fine examples are featured on many of the following page spreads.

Clan surnames

When clan surnames were introduced into English, they were translated from Gaelic – thus some people called MacGregor became Gregorson, some MacHendries became Henderson, some MacPatricks became Paterson, and

Some Scandinavian surnames were also formed in this manner. Names such as Magnusson, Hendriksson or Haraldsson illustrate this. We also get Norman surnames like Fitzclarence, Fitzwilliam, Fitzroy, Fitzjames. Fitz means 'son

Where can we find the clans?

Was the clan system only in the Scottish Highlands? Or was the division between the Highland and Lowland way of life less clear cut?

After all, Lowlanders had borrowed from Highland social customs and vice versa for many centuries. Scotland has been one country for over 1000 years.

Clans once existed all over Scotland, but they lasted far longer in the Gaelic-speaking Highlands than anywhere else. In the Scots-speaking Lowlands, however, the kings of Scotland, who were based there, soon got rid of them.

So the heartland of the clan system was and remains the Highlands. The Highland Region, as it is known today, is the area north and west of the 'Highland line', a landscape of high rugged mountains and deep straths and glens. The Highland Region includes more than half the land area of Scotland, and up until 1750 half of its population.

The clan system lasted in the Highlands until it was crushed after Bonnie Prince Charlie's Jacobite Rebellion of 1745. Before that time, clan communities were scattered

Bonnie Prince Charlie

Charles Edward Stuart, known as 'Bonnie Prince Charlie', was the son of the exiled James Francis Edward, whose father had been James VII of Scotland and II of England and Ireland. Charles, the 'Young Pretender', came back to Scotland in 1745, determined to reclaim the throne for his father. At the Battle of Culloden in April 1746, the Protestant government troops defeated Charles' army, setting in motion a series of acts and laws that would crush the clan system as a way of life.

thinly through the hilly landscape, and clan territories were defended fiercely by their chiefs. Indeed, it was because so many chiefs were able to call out their own private armies of clansmen in support of Bonnie Prince Charlie in 1745 that the government in London decided to crush the clan system.

Outside the Highlands, the clan system had died out as a way of life by about the 14th century in the Lowlands, and by the 16th century in Galloway and the Borders.

The Glenfinnan Monument (below) was built at the head of Loch Shiel, Lochaber, in 1815. Charles Edward Stuart raised his standard in this spot to mark the beginning of the 1745 Jacobite Rebellion.

Dress Stewart

Scotland's private army

Find out where you can still see the only private army in Britain (shown above). This regiment is descended from the clansmen called out long ago by the chiefs of what clan? Nowadays it is only used for ceremonial occasions.

Answer on page 40

BLAIR CASTLE

The code of the Highland clans

What language did the clan members speak?

Most Highland clansmen spoke **Gaelic**, one of the **Celtic** languages, and not **Scots**. They saw themselves as a family, descended from one ancestor, rather than a group of peasants ruled by a lord. The chief was usually an educated man, who spoke Scots as well as Gaelic. When necessary, he spoke on behalf of his people to the Scots-speaking king or queen of Scotland in far-away Edinburgh, or later to the English-speaking ruler of the united crown of Scotland and England in even further-off London.

The chief was often a tyrant, but his people relied on him for leadership in times of danger.

The chief leased out the clan's lands to his relations and to the warrior leaders. These were his **tacksmen** (or chief tenants). They in turn rented smaller parcels of land out to tenants and to **cottars** (or sub-tenants). Rents were paid in goods and military service, but not in money. Even in the 18th century, MacDonald of Keppoch, for example, claimed that his 'rent-roll' was 500 fighting men.

Within this system, the poorest clansmen could feel part of the same family as the chief. After all, they all had the same name. If you were all MacLeods or MacDonalds, you would have a deep sense of your clan's shared history, blood, territory and honour. You would be proud to respect and obey your chief, because to you he was a wise father acting in the best interests of your whole clan family. It was this blood kinship, real or imagined, that was unique to the Highland clans.

Left: A Highland shepherd in a late 18th-century style of dress. This was the kind of clothes adopted by shepherds and drovers – men who were mostly on the move in their line of work.

Mystery object

Do you know what this is?
A clue – it was vital piece of
kit for a Highland fighting man.

Answer on page 40

The clans, however, often had a reputation for lawlessness, and relations between them were often bad. Raiding another clan's land and stealing their goods – and even their people – were common events. There are many stories of bitter feuds, petty jealousies and terrible atrocities committed by one clan against another. Cattle-raiding especially led to many a clan battle.

MacDonald of Keppoch

While the Lowlands of Scotland slowly developed into a place where people obeyed the king and the law, the Highland chiefs remained beyond the monarch's power. The chiefs often acted like minor kings. If clansmen had to choose between the king or queen's commands and those of their chief, it was often the royal command which was ignored. And because the clans were scattered over difficult country, monarchs found themselves unable to punish them.

Clan weapons

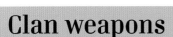

On this page you will find a number of fine examples of the craft of weaponry. Above is a silver-plated Highland flintlock pistol made in Doune, near Stirling, by T. Murdoch in the 18th century. These 'Doune pistols' were popular with Highlanders and many who carried them were involved in the Jacobite uprisings of 1715 and '45.

The sword (right) is a Highland basket-hilted weapon. It has an inscription on its blade in support of the Jacobite cause (see page 27).

The knives (above), known as dirks, date from the 17th to 18th century. The handles were usually made from wood, but sometimes other materials like bone, or were bound with leather strips.

Clan names

Below: Evidence of Scandinavian influence on clan culture is illustrated by such objects as this slate carving. It was found at Jarlshof, a Norse settlement on Shetland.

How did the clans create their distinctive names? They were created in four main ways –

Patronymics

A surname based on the father's name was called a **patronymic**. It was created by putting the prefix 'Mac-' in front of the name, meaning 'son of' in Gaelic. In English-speaking clans, the suffix '-son' is placed after the name. Most clan surnames were created in this way. Examples include such names as MacNeil, MacCallum, MacAlister, MacDonald, MacEwen, Farquharson, Fergusson, Nicholson, Morrison, Robertson.

Occupational names

These surnames revealed the clan ancestor's job or trade, such as MacPherson as 'son of the parson', MacIntosh as 'son of the chieftain', MacIntyre as 'son of the carpenter', MacMaster as 'son of the master' (that is the priest), and MacSporran as 'son of the purse-bearer'.

Territorial names

Such surnames were based on where the clan came from, like Murray, Ross, Sutherland, Lennox or Ruthven.

Nicknames

These suggested what an ancestor looked like, or what kind of temper he had –

Grant	'big'
Cameron	'crooked nose'
Campbell	'crooked mouth'

Surname search

Find out the meaning of your surname? Your local library should have a dictionary of surnames to help you, or go online at:

www.surnames.behindthename.com

MacDuff	'son of the dark one'
MacIlroy	'son of the red-haired lad'
MacGillivray	'son of the servant of good judgement'

Farquharson

Shetland Islands

However, not all clan names were taken from the Gaelic language. Some were from **Scandinavian** sources (Gunn, MacLeod, MacCorquodale), some were **Pictish** (Brodie, Moncrieff), some were **Norman** (Grant, Fraser, Sinclair), and some were from **Strathclyde Britons** (Galbraith, Campbell).

Over the centuries, some clans went from speaking only Gaelic to speaking English, and changed their names accordingly – MacRobert, for example, became Robertson, MacFarquhar became Farquharson, MacMorris became Morrison, and so on. Other clansmen, especially after the 1745 Jacobite Rebellion, dropped 'Mac-' from their names altogether, and surnames like Andrew, Arthur, Donald and Kinnon appeared.

Scotland in the 7th to 9th centuries

To the right is a map that charts the settlements of different peoples around the time of the Celtic period.

VIKINGS

NORTHERN PICTS

SOUTHERN PICTS

SCOTS

ANGLES

BRITONS

NIDUARI PICTS

Evidence of Pictish influence in Scotland can be seen in this impressive **broch** construction in the background. The stone harper carving (far left) is also Pictish. It was found in Monifieth, Angus.

11

The Gaelic language

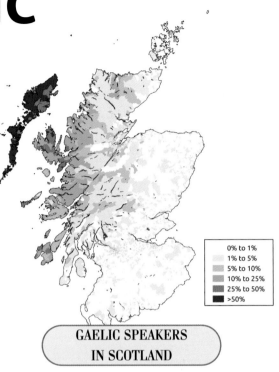

GAELIC SPEAKERS IN SCOTLAND

Key:
- 0% to 1%
- 1% to 5%
- 5% to 10%
- 10% to 25%
- 25% to 50%
- >50%

What are the origins of the Gaelic language and how did it become the language of the clans?

Gaelic has been spoken for longer than any other known language in Scotland. It first reached Argyll from Ireland in the 4th century AD. By the ninth century it had taken over from the Pictish culture and language of northern Scotland, to which it was related. It also overwhelmed the Norse language of the Scandinavian invaders of Scotland's west coast.

Gaelic was at its peak in Scotland between the 9th and the 13th centuries. It has always been strongest in the north and west of Scotland.

Although the clan system was not limited to the Gaelic-speaking Highlands, it survived longest there. It is for this reason that today we think of Gaelic as the language of the clans.

> The map above shows the geographic spread of Gaelic speakers in Scotland, when the last Census was carried out in 2011. The key highlights the percentage of Gaelic speakers within the population as a whole in these areas.

Gaelic first names

Did you know that many first names come from Gaelic sources? Here are a few of them (Gaelic spellings first, English in brackets).

Boys' names

Alasdair, Aonghas (Angus), Calum, Diarmid, Dughall (Dougal), Eoghann (Ewan), Fearghas (Fergus), Fionnlagh (Finlay), Iain (Ian), Lachlann (Lachlan), Murchadh (Murdo), Niall (Neil), Raghnall (Ranald), Ruairidh (Rory), Seumas (Hamish), Somhairle (Sorley), Torcall (Torquil)

Girls' names

Catriona, Ciorstag (Kirsty), Deirdre, Eithne, Iseabail (Ishbel), Mairi (Mary), Moire (Moira), Morag, Morna, Rona, Seonaid (Shona), Sine (Sheena), Sile (Sheila)

Scottish place-names

Did you know that many Scottish placenames are from Gaelic? Work out what some of these place-names mean by looking at the table. Note that adjective qualifiers follow their nouns in Gaelic unlike English:

Ballochbuie Kilcreggan
Ben More Kilpatrick
Braemar Kinlochleven
Dundonald Kyles of Bute
Inchkenneth Strathspey
Inverness Tobermory

Answers on page 40

MAP SPELLING	GAELIC	MEANING
balloch	bealach	pass
bar	bàrr	top, summit
beg	beag	small (not big!)
ben	beinn	mountain, hill
brae	bràighe	upland
buie	buidhe	yellow
craig	creag	hill, rock, crag
drum	druim	ridge of a hill
dun	dùn	hill-fortress, castle
eccles, eagles	eaglais/eagas	church (not eagles!)
glen	gleann	glen or valley
inch	innis	island
inver	inbhir	river-mouth
kil	cill	monk's cell, church
kin	ceann	head, top
kyle	caol	narrow strait
loch	loch	loc
more	mòr	big
mory	moire/mhoire	of Mary
strath	srath	broad valley
tober	tobar	well

SAILM DHAIBHIDH

A Meadar Dhàna Gaoidheilg, Do rèir na Heabhra:

Agus na tranflàfioin is feart a Mbéarla agus a Nlaidin, do thionnfgnadh le *Seanàdh* EARRAGHAOIDHEAL fan bhliadhna 1659, agus anois air a ntabhairt gu crìch, do chum gu dèanta an feinm a Neaglaifaibh agus a dteaghlachaibh a' ghnàthuigheas an chànamhain fin.

Col. 3. 16.

Biodh focàl Chriofd na chomhnuidhe ionruibh gu faidhbhir fa nuile ghliocas ar dteagafg, agus ar munadh dhiobh a chéile a Salmaibh, agus a bhfonnaibh molta Dé, agus a gceainticaibh Spioradalta an dèanamh ...

M. DCC. VII.

The Gaelic Bible

A Scottish Gaelic version of the Bible first appeared in London in 1690, written by the Reverend Robert Kirk, minister at Aberfoyle. A more widely-used translation came out in 1767, however. This was a New Testament compiled by Dr James Stuart and Dugald Buchanan.

A830
Gleann Fhionnainn / Glenfinnan 5
Ceann Loch Àilleart / Lochailort 14
Àrasaig / Arisaig 24
Malaig / Mallaig 34

13

The clan seat

Clan histories cover a very long timespan; many clans began as far back as the 13th century.

Thus the clan's seat – or its centre of power – often followed the fortunes of the family, moving up and down the land to grander or more modest locations. Most Scottish castles therefore have links with more than one clan. Only a few, like Dunvegan, have remained in the hands of one family.

The clan chief's castle became the seat of the clan. It was not just a defensive fortress; it was often a mini-court too, and the chief's important officials worked here. You can read about the clan chief's harpers, pipers, bards, clerks and pursers in the following pages.

This bow brooch, dated to 300-100 BC, is made from copper alloy decorated with enamelling. It came from the excavations at Finlaggan.

The *breithearch* (or brieve or judge) administered the laws of the clan here. Like so many clan positions, this office was often held by one family, passing from father to son.

Some clan chiefs lived in great style. In the 14th and 15th centuries, the MacDonald Lords of the Isles kept a huge civil service for almost the entire Western Isles from their base at now-ruined Finlaggan on Islay.

Finlaggan

Archaeologists have now finished excavating this site, but not before making some very interesting discoveries, such as the beautiful brooch featured on the opposite page.

Today many clan seats are the nerve centres of worldwide family networks. Clansmen from the farthest corners of the world gather together in fellowship from time to time at the invitation of their chief. These gatherings have helped to keep the clan idea alive through the 20th century and into the 21st.

Take a look at the castles pictured here. Which ones have you visited? Have they any links with any particular clans?

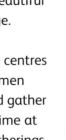

Urquhart

Some clan seats

CASTLE	LOCATION	CLAN
Brodie	near Forres	Brodie
Duart	Isle of Mull	MacLean of Duart
Dunvegan	Isle of Skye	MacLeod of MacLeod
Ferniehirst	near Jedburgh	Kerr
Huntly	Huntly	Gordon
Inveraray	Inveraray	Campbell
Kisimul	Isle of Barra	MacNeil of Barra
Menzies	near Aberfeldy	Menzies
Tioram	Ardnamurchan	MacDonald of Clanranald
Urquhart	near Drumnadrochit	Urquhart

BRODIE CASTLE

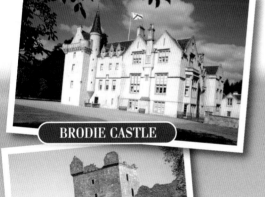

URQUHART CASTLE

Eilean Donan at Dornie, once the seat of Clan MacRae, and later the MacRaes on behalf of the Mackenzie chiefs, was destroyed and abandoned after the Jacobite Rebellion and rebuilt during the 20th century.

15

The Highland clan chief

Loyalty to the chief was the key to being a clansman or clanswoman. The early chiefs could do no wrong, and were almost gods in the eyes of their clan.

The chief was the protector and custodian of the clan's territory. He made the laws for the clan, and clansfolk were bound to accept his authority over them. He was the leader of his people and the clansmen were his private army in time of war.

The figure on the right of this panel is wearing a mail coat over a quilted linen coat and the pointed helmet of a Gaelic chieftain. The panel comes from the tomb of Alexander MacLeod in St Clement's Church, Rodel, Harris, and it dates to c.1528.

Over the years, of course, the role of the chief changed greatly – as greatly as clan society itself changed. From being the custodian and defender of clan territory, the chief became its owner – and landlord.

After 1600, more and more of the chiefs' eldest sons were educated in English – by orders of the king. The chiefs were the first of their clans to move in two very different societies – Gaelic-speaking clan society, and English-speaking Lowland Scotland and England.

Some chiefs spent most of their time away from their clans, and lost touch with their people's needs and problems.

MacNeil

By the 19th century, the London government ruled England, Ireland and Scotland through the Lords-Lieutenant of the various counties. In the Highlands this system fitted awkwardly with the clan system and with Gaelic social customs. A story is told about the great MacDonald chief who was invited to dine with the Lord-Lieutenant of Argyll. An apology was made to the chief for seating him so far away from the head of the table. 'Where The MacDonald sits,' came the proud response, '*there* is the head of the table.'

Eilean Sith (Kisimul Castle), Castlebay, Isle of Barra.

Family tales

The following story is told of an eccentric MacNeil chieftain. After dinner each evening, his steward was instructed to cry from the battlements of Kisimul Castle, 'The MacNeil of Barra having dined, the peoples of the earth may now eat.'

And in the Bible story of Noah's Ark, one of the ancestors of this chief was said to have refused Noah's hospitality 'because The MacNeil of Barra has a boat of his own'. Do you have a humorous story to tell about the head of your family?

Harpers and pipers

Two occupations of the clansmen involved making music. In early times, the harp-player was an important official in the household of many clan chiefs. Another key role was that of the piper.

Gaelic harp, dated to c.1500, from the National Museum of Scotland.

The office of **harper** or **piper** was often a hereditary one, handed down from father to son. Sometimes farms were attached to the job, and even today you may come across steadings called Harperfield or Harpercroft.

The Gaelic word for harp is *clarsach*, and there are pictures of harps on Pictish stones from as long ago as the 8th century. After 1603 there were no Royal harpers at court, but many chiefs continued to employ them until the 18th century. One of the most famous musicians was Roderick Morrison of Bragar in Lewis. He was called the 'blind harper' and he died about 1713. Morrison was also a **bard** or clan poet. You can find out more about bards on page 20.

The post of piper was often passed from father to son in one family. Most chiefs had a piper. Famous family pipers included the

MacCrimmons, who were pipers to the MacLeod chieftains on Skye for over 200 years. MacCrimmon piping was considered so marvellous that people used to say that the family had learned their skills from the fairies. In fact, they had a school of piping at Boreraig, near Dunvegan, until 1770.

Medal awarded for piping at the Lochaber Gathering of 1885.

18

Mystery object

Can you guess what this object is?
A clue – it's not the way that you
usually look at this object.

Answer on page 40

Paying the piper!

A common saying from clan life is known
nowadays to English speakers worldwide.
Do you know what it means?

'He who pays the piper calls the tune.'

Answer on page 40

The Laird of Grant's piper

When the last MacCrimmon piper was
preparing to emigrate to Canada around
1800, he got no farther than Greenock. His
love of Skye prevented him from embarking
on the ship. He returned to his beloved island,
where he died in 1822, aged 91.

It was these hereditary pipers who created
pibroch or classical bagpipe music. The
forms were developed from one generation
to another. **Pibroch** is taken from Gaelic
piobaireachd, meaning playing pipes.

Then, as today, musicians often held
competitions to see who was the best – it
was a good way to keep standards high!

This famous picture of *William Cumming, Piper
to the Laird of Grant*, was painted by Richard
Watt in 1714. Cumming has all the trappings of
his feudal chieftain – a banner, coat of arms and
tartan livery. The banner shows the Grant clan
slogan, 'Stand Fast!', sometimes 'Stand Fast,
Craigellachie!' – the name of a hill which served
as a gathering place in times of crisis.

19

Bards, clerks and pursers

Important clan chiefs often kept a large household to help them run clan society. The richer and more successful the clan, the bigger the chief's household.

This wooden quaich, or drinking cup, belonged to the Gaelic bard known as Rob Donn MacKay (1714-78), a Sutherland poet of the oral tradition. Because he could not read or write, his work was written down by a neighbour.

Some of the most important people were the **pursers** (purse-bearers) who looked after the clan's money, the **clerks** who did any writing and reading that was required, and the **bards** who composed, recited or sang poems for the clan. These offices were often hereditary – passed down across the generations from father to son. Their occupations give us such surnames as MacSporran ('son of the purse-keeper') and MacCleary or MacCleery ('son of the clerk').

The bards often told stories in their poems. Long ago, some of these stories were taken from Celtic legends and Irish sagas, with tales of the heroic deeds of Finn MacCool, the adventures of Cuchulain and of Ossian. There were hundreds of these stories, and the bards told and retold them to entertain and to instruct the clansfolk. These groups of stories were called **cycles** – the **Fenian cycle** and the **Ulster cycle** were the most famous. Listening to the cycles, the clansfolk would get to know the main character over many episodes, and they looked forward to hearing about their next adventures.

The *Gàidhealtachd*

This image shows a bard and harper performing at a feast in Ireland in the sixteenth century. The bards and harpers were members of the learned orders of the *Gàidhealtachd* (or Gaelic-speaking area) in Ireland and in Scotland, and were held in deepest respect as teachers of the art of poetry, as well as grammar, language, law, history, genealogy and Latin.

The bards were the clan poets of Gaelic society. During the clan chief's life they wrote **praise poems** for him, and when he died they lamented his passing. They also praised the clan's territory and composed warrior chants. The bards were often very important men, owning good land and property.

MacIntyre

Praise poem

Here is an 18th-century bard's praise poem to a local landmark:

The Praise of Ben Dorain

*Over mountains, pride
Of place to Ben Dorain!
I've nowhere espied
A finer to reign.
In her moorbacks wide
Hosts of shy deer bide
While light comes pouring
Diamond-wise from her side.*

This is the 20th-century **Hugh MacDiarmid**'s translation of a verse of a famous Gaelic praise poem by the bard **Duncan Ban MacIntyre** (1724-1812)

Why don't you try to write a praise poem? It doesn't have to rhyme, but it does have to praise a person or a place.

Ossian

James Macpherson (left) (1736-96) published his *Fragments of Ancient Poetry, Collected in the Highlands of Scotland* in 1760 and made the Gaelic writing tradition very popular throughout Britain and Europe. His work was translated into all the main languages of Europe, including French (as the title page above illustrates).

Galloway and Border clans

Below: This enormous cannon – the biggest in Scotland – was used to great effect by King James II against the mighty Douglas clan. Do you know what is it called? And where can you see it today?

Answer on page 40

The hilly province of Galloway in south-west Scotland was always fiercely independent. It was hard for Scots kings and queens to keep law and order there.

The Kennedys (in Carrick), the Macdowalls and Agnews (in Wigtownshire), the Irvines and Maxwells (in Nithsdale), the Bruces and Johnstones (in Annandale) – these were all clans in former times.

For hundreds of years, the hilly Border counties of Berwick, Roxburgh, Selkirk, Peebles and Dumfries were a law unto themselves. For a start, this was the border line for two nations. If life got too difficult for lawbreakers on the Scottish side of the Borders up to 1603, it was easy enough for them to slip off into England until things quietened down at home.

When England invaded Scotland, it was through this countryside that the English soldiers marched. Border families like the Kerrs and Humes, Elliots and Hays, Armstrongs and Scotts were needed to defend Scotland against England. Thus it was in the Scottish king or queen's interest to let them keep their weapons.

THE DEVIL'S BEEF TUB, near MOFFAT

The people of the Borders spoke Scots, but in many respects they behaved like the Gaelic-speaking Highlanders. They too were loyal to their chief and defended their territory. And for them **reiving** – thieving and plundering for food, mainly cattle – was a popular occupation.

The Devil's Beef Tub, near Moffat at the head of Annandale, got its name because it was used as a reivers' hideout – the 'beef' being stolen cattle and the 'tub' a well-hidden valley.

In the 16th century, the powerful Armstrong family was said to be able to raise 3000 horsemen. King James V saw them as a threat to his royal authority. According to tradition, the king tricked Johnnie Armstrong of Gilnockie (near Langholm) to attend a meeting with him at Hawick, only to have him hanged there without trial in 1529. Another Armstrong laird was hanged in 1610 for reiving in Cumberland.

For a long time, it seemed as if there were two codes of conduct in the Borders. When

Bruce

the monarch and the government based in Edinburgh were strong, the power of the local chiefs was kept in check. But when the central government was weak – as it often was – the local chiefs were left to rule the roost. However, through time, the Borders chieftains began to lose their power.

King James V of Scotland (1512-42), who sent a letter to the reiver Johnnie Armstrong, inviting him to attend the court at Hawick.

Johnnie Armstrong

John Armstrong of Gilnockie may have been treacherously assassinated by King James V in 1529, along with 36 of his followers, but that wasn't the end of the Armstrong story. His relative, William Armstrong, known as 'Kinmont Willie', continued to disregard the authority of the Scots and the English kings. The ballad of

'Kinmont Willie' is well retold by Sir Walter Scott in his *Minstrelsy of the Scottish Border*, and it describes some famous episodes of skullduggery and derring-do.

Lowland clans and families

Even in the Lowlands, the influence of the clan system can easily be seen.

Fife and Stirling were in fact regarded as being in 'the Highlands' until the 16th century. This was perhaps because they had once been part of the Pictish kingdom.

Glasgow itself was a half-Highland town until after this time, with Gaelic spoken in the surrounding areas, such as Greenock, Dumbarton and Drymen, right into the 19th century.

This late 17th-century painting (below) shows the celebration of a wedding in the Lowlands of Scotland. The bridal couple (centre) lead the dance to the tune of the piper, while the rest of the guests look on.

It is therefore unsurprising that families such as Buchanan, Elphinstone, Lennox, Galbraith (in Stirlingshire), Boyd, Montgomery, Cunningham, Wallace (in Ayrshire), Crawford, Carmichael (Lanarkshire), Dundas, Crichton, Borthwick (Lothian) behaved in some ways like the Highland clans in earlier times, before they became locked into the Scottish kingdom.

Lowland

Clan versus king

Why do you suppose that the clans never united against the King of Scots?

Answer on page 40

Buchanan

time were pretending they had nothing in common with their Highland cousins. They were too busy looking towards the south and modelling themselves carefully on English society. Many Lowlanders didn't even call themselves Scots any more. They labelled themselves 'North British'.

Other semi-clannish Lowland families included Arbuthnott, Graham, Ogilvie in Tayside; Lesley, Primrose in Fife; Moncreiffe, Haldane, Rollo in Strathearn; Swinton and Nesbit in Berwickshire.

You can almost imagine the clan chiefs as a set of dominoes falling to the Scottish crown. The first dominoes to fall were in Lothian, and they in turn knocked down others throughout the Lowlands. By the 18th century the clan system had retreated behind the Highland line. Lowlanders by this

Below is the painting *Highland Dance*, by the Scottish artist David Allan. It is dated to the late 18th century. These guests at a wedding near Blair Atholl are wearing tartan as a suitably smart fashion for the occasion. This taste for wearing tartan survived the years of banishment after the Jacobite Rebellion (see pages 26-27).

Highland

Clans in the 18th century

Throughout history it has always been difficult for two or more cultures to co-exist peacefully within one country.

General George Wade (1673-1748) (above) and Thomas Telford (1757-1834) drove fine new roads across the Highlands, making the area much more accessible.

With massive English backing, Scotland solved the problem of its two cultures in the 18th century. Between 1700 and 1800, the Gaelic-speaking clan society of the High-lands was destroyed as a working culture.

The Scots Parliament in Edinburgh and, after the Union between Scotland and England in 1707, the British Parliament in London, were very frightened of the clans and their power. Government policy was introduced to break the power of the chiefs and subdue the Highlands.

The government built fortresses and sent soldiers to man them to keep the clans in check. You can still see these fortresses today at Fort Augustus and at Fort George near Inverness, the Ruthven Barracks on Speyside, and Bernera Barracks at Glenelg near the Kyle of Lochalsh. Corgarff Castle in Upper Donside, Aberdeenshire, was restored for government soldiers. Roads, bridges, harbours and canals were also built in the Highlands so that troops could be quickly moved around to deal with trouble.

Acts against the clans

Here are some of the acts that the government passed to control the Highlanders:

- **The Clan Act** (1715) – designed to break the ties between the chief and his men.
- **The Disarming Acts** (1716 and 1725) – which imposed fines on the possession of weapons, allowing searches to be carried out and weapons seized.
- **The Proscription Act** (1746) – which out-lawed the wearing of the kilt and tartan until 1782.
- **The Annexing Act** (1752) turned the land of Jacobite supporters into crown lands, managed by crown commissioners.

Jacobitism

In 1692 a terrible plot had been hatched by the government. It was decided that by slaughtering members of one clan, other clans would be frightened into abandoning the Jacobite cause. This resulted in the violent massacre of MacDonald clansmen at Glencoe on the chilly morning of 13 February. Campbell of Glenlyon (with government troops) killed men, women and children alike. And what was the government's excuse? The MacDonald chief, due to bad weather, had been a few days late in signing an oath of allegiance to the king.

After the Battle of Culloden in April 1746, when Bonnie Prince Charlie left for France and a life in exile, the government punished the Jacobite rebels and introduced more Acts to crush the clans. Over time the clan system was broken up and people moved away from the land in search of work and food in the cities of the Lowlands.

After 1746, and during the 19th century, the government implemented land reform and many crofters were cleared off the land to make way for sheep. During what was to become known as the **Highland Clearances**, more than 100,000 clansfolk left their homes for North America.

Did you know?

More clansmen supported the Hanoverian (government) side than the Jacobite (rebel) cause during the 1745 Rebellion. Yet the government persisted in treating the Highlands as if everyone living there supported the Jacobites.

The Clearances were often achieved only by considerable violence towards women, children and old folk, who naturally did not wish to leave their homes or to break up their families.

BONNIE PRINCE CHARLIE

Clans in the 19th century

After the 18th century, clan chiefs were no longer capable of raising armies. This helped to destroy traditional clan society.

Queen Victoria wrote a book entitled *Leaves from the Journal of our Life in the Highlands* (1868), created after the death of her beloved husband Prince Albert. The book became very popular and helped to bring thousands of visitors to 'Royal Deeside'.

By the 19th century, people throughout Britain began to take a scholarly interest in Gaeldom and the clans. Now that it was no longer considered a threat to them, people outside the Highlands were very interested to see how the clan system had worked.

Dr Samuel Johnson, the London wit and scholar, appreciated Highland culture. He visited the ruined abbey of Iona in 1773 in the company of the chief of the clan MacLean of Duart. His travels with James Boswell are recorded in the latter's *Journal of a Tour to the Hebrides* (1785), one of the first great travel books.

The author Walter Scott (1771-1832) was particularly important in spreading interest in the clans. His writings described the clash of Gaelic clan culture with that of Lowland Scotland. Novels like *Waverley*, *Old Mortality* and *Rob Roy* dramatise this subject and were enormous bestsellers in their day.

Inspired by the fictional accounts, a steady stream of distinguished visitors came to the Scottish Highlands. As well as Robert Burns and Walter Scott, English writers such as Dr Samuel Johnson and William Wordsworth, and the German composer Felix Mendelssohn, admired the wildness of the landscape and enjoyed the civilised company of the clan chiefs.

But the greatest enthusiasm for the Highland clans came about as a result of the state visit of King George IV to Edinburgh in 1822. This was the first visit of a reigning

British monarch to the northern kingdom in 171 years. The clan chiefs in full Highland dress were presented to the king at Holyroodhouse, with the king himself dressed in a kilt. Many of these ceremonial events were stage managed by Walter Scott.

Queen Victoria was the British monarch who did most to restore dignity to Highland culture. She made her first visit to the region in 1842 and fell in love with the place and the people. She was very conscious of her own Stuart ancestry. Victoria bought an estate at Balmoral, Aberdeenshire, and it became her base for royal journeys throughout the Highlands. She also encouraged tartan-weaving and boosted the Harris tweed industry, setting a fashion for the hard-wearing cloth. Her diaries of Highland life were also to become bestsellers.

The tourist trail

Soon the travel entrepreneur Thomas Cook was using the new railway network to organise tours of the Highlands. The area has become a firm favourite for tourism, sports, hill-walking, mountaineering and back-packing ever since.

Clans and Empire

The British Army provided a lifeline for clan culture when it was most needed. Just when the power of the clan chiefs was being broken, new Highland regiments were formed for service in the rapidly expanding British Empire.

Impoverished clansmen enlisted in their thousands. The regiment was more than their livelihood – it became a substitute for the clan itself and clan chiefs were often the officers.

The kilt

The kilt worn today is the ***feileadh beag*** or **philabeg**, or 'little kilt'. The ***feileadh mor*** or 'big kilt', the cloak version, is no longer in use.

The traditional dress of all Highland men – rich or poor, chieftain or clansman – was a shirt and a **plaid** or blanket worn over it, with the legs bare. The **plaid** was simple to make and wear, and was a width of tartan cloth several yards in length. Like the Indian *sari*, it had to be carefully arranged. It was worn as a loose cloak, gathered at the waist by a leather belt. Below the belt it was pleated, and it reached down almost to the knees. Above the belt it could be worn like a cloak over the shoulders to keep out the cold or wet. If the weather was fine, it could be draped down over the belt to cover the legs. At night it made a good blanket.

Above and below are illustrations that show how versatile the kilt could be. The soldiers (above) often used the upper corner of the belted plaid to keep their muskets dry.

Up until the 17th century, Lowlanders and foreign visitors to Scotland regarded the dress of Highland men as a sort of exotic uniform. But by the 18th century, as a result of the Jacobite rebellions, the distinctive kilted uniforms of Highland soldiers had become quite widely recognised outside the Highlands.

After the Battle of Culloden, an Act was passed by Parliament which outlawed the wearing of Highland dress and tartan for almost 40 years. Anyone caught wearing a kilt faced trans-portation 'beyond the seas … for the space of seven years'.

But the kilt did survive, because recruits to the new Highland regiments of the British Army (see pages 32-33) were kitted out in this distinctive fashion. Regiments such as the Black Watch and Seaforth Highlanders ensured that the wearing of the kilt and the use of tartan continued. The Act forbidding the wearing of the kilt was repealed in the year 1782.

By 1822, when King George IV visited Edinburgh, the kilt had become very fashionable and the king himself wore one. The seal of approval for the kilt finally came in the 1840s when Queen Victoria fell in love with the Highlands and Highland culture (see pages 28-29).

Today the kilt is worn by all Scots, Lowlanders and Highlanders alike. It is now a symbol not just of Highland clan identity, but of Scottish identity.

Highland women in the 18th century wore a plaid shawl, called an *earasaid* or *arisaid*, usually of tartan. This illustration came from *The Clans of the Scottish Highlands*, a book published in 1845/47 by James Logan and R. R. McIan. Although based on historical research, their work added to the growing myth of clan tartans. This woman is wearing the tartan of the Sinclair clan.

Balmoral

Specially designed by Prince Albert in the 1850s, the **sett** or pattern of this tartan was based on the so-called **Royal Stewart**, but in shades of marled grey. It was said to represent the rugged Grampian peaks.

Sporran

The kilt of course had no pockets, hence the need for a **sporran** – a sort of purse or pouch worn on the belt of the kilt.

Design your own sporrans for (1) everyday use; and (2) for wearing to a wedding or special event.

List the materials you might use to make these sporrans.

Name your tartan

Today's kilts come in different tartans, and most clans have their own tartan. Is your name linked to a clan and a tartan? You can find out online at:

www.scotshistoryonline.co.uk/ tartan-history.html

or by visiting the **Tartans of Scotland** website at:
www.tartans.scotland.net

Tartan

Today's tartans, with their bright colours and special patterns for different clans, are not old.

Checked cloth was woven from early times in Scotland. Dark and light shades of wool were woven together in regular patterns. The wool came originally from goat-like sheep. Vegetable dyes were used, such as leaves, berries, tree bark and lichens. Brambles gave blue dye, blueberries purple, alder tree bark gave black, birch bark gave yellow, and so on. The **sett** or design of a tartan differed from one place to another, and from one weaver to another.

At the Battle of Killiecrankie (1689), Glengarry's men wore scarlet hose and plaids crossed with a purple stripe, Cameron of Lochiel was in a coat of three colours, while the plaid of MacNeil of Barra 'rivalled the rainbow'.

Most of today's tartans date from the 19th century, when people became interested in Highland culture once again (see pages 28-29). At that time, the main designers and manufacturers of tartan cloth were the large firms of weavers set up to supply cloth for army regiments and private customers. The most famous of these firms was Wilson's of Bannockburn, whose early order books show us what patterns were like at the time.

The Falkirk tartan

This fragment of woven cloth was excavated in Falkirk. It dates to the 3rd century AD. The fabric uses two shades of natural wool in a contrasting pattern. Below is a reproduction of the twill weave to show how the check pattern was created.

Regimental tartans, like the Black Watch, had a big influence on today's clan tartans. The Black Watch tartan was even adopted as the Campbell clan tartan because so many Campbells used to serve in the regiment. Gordon, Mackenzie and Robertson tartans also have their origins in the British Army.

Mystery object

This object was created to show off nature's contribution to fashion. Can you guess what it is?

Answer on page 40

Gordon

Tartan societies

People wear tartan today to show their clan or family identity. Descendants of Highland families live all over the world, but they can still proclaim their Scottish identity by donning the colours of their clan.

New tartans can still be registered with National Archives of Scotland's

Scottish Register of Tartans at: **www.tartanregister.gov.uk**

The Register contains thousands of tartan designs, which are free for you to search and reference.

Above: A detail from a recruitment poster for the Gordon Highlanders.

Right: Tartan fabric is internationally famous today. However, as this advertisement from 1880 shows, it has been popular in Parisian fashion houses and in the world of *haute couture* for many years.

Celtic connections

A recently registered tartan (2010) was created for the island of Ouessant in Brittany. Like Scotland, Brittany still celebrates its Celtic culture. The sett includes black and white from the Breton flag, red and yellow from the island's crest, and blue and green to celebrate the ancient robes of the Celtic druids and bards.

Clan slogans

Below: Most Highland clans had an ancient gathering ground. Long ago, when the clan was threatened, a clansman would carry a fiery cross from their ground, throughout the clan lands, shouting the clan slogan. All clansmen would then know to come to the gathering ground.

Advertising agencies are paid lots of money to dream up distinctive slogans and catchphrases for businesses and manufacturers.

Most English-language speakers know what a slogan is. What is not often known is that the word **slogan** comes from Gaelic *sluagh-ghairm*. Originally it meant a war-cry or rallying cry, and it was used by clansmen as a password or signal in battle. Each clan had a different slogan, and it was often the name of their chief or a famous ancestor, or sometimes their clan seat. A password was another way for clansmen to recognise each other; this could prove very useful if you were fighting in the dark.

In 1689 an English visitor to the Scottish Borders wrote about the slogan or battle-cry of the Hume clan: 'The Name of Hume have it for their Slughorn [slogan], *A Hume, a Hume!*'

Clan slogans

Here are a few examples of the *sluagh-ghairm*, or **slogan**, of the Highland clans:

CLAN	GAELIC *SLUAGH-GHAIRM*	ENGLISH MEANING
Buchanan	Clar Innis	Island name, on Loch Lomond
Cameron	Chlanna nan con thigibh 's geibh sibh feoil	Sons of the hounds, come and get flesh!
Grant	Creag Eileachaidh	Stand fast, Craigellachie! [rocky landmark on Speyside]
MacDonald of Keppoch	Dia 's Naomh Aindrea	God and Saint Andrew!
MacDougall	Buaidh no Bas	Victory or death!
Mackay	Bratach bhan mhic Aoidh	White banner of Mackay
Mackinnon	Cuihnich bas Ailpein	Remember the death of Alpin!
MacLean	Fear eile airson Eachuinn	Another [fighter] for Hector!

Make up your own slogan. It could be based on a place you like, or it could be a grisly threat like that of the Camerons. When might you use your slogan?

Cameron

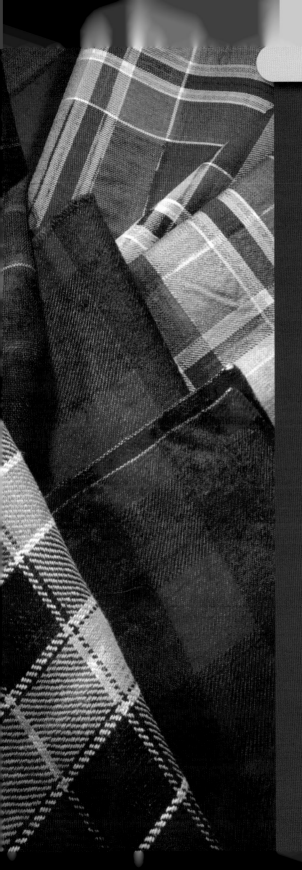

Clan badges and plants

The wearing of tartan and the kilt was forbidden by law during the period 1746-82, but that did not stop clansfolk from revealing their true identity.

Long before the days of modern tartans, clansfolk wore their chief's crest badge and also the clan plant as means of identification. These were worn on the cap, although the plant is now seen more often as a button-hole. They were two easy ways for clansmen to state their clan identity, especially during the time when tartan and kilt-wearing were banned.

The clan plant was something that grew well in the clan's territory. But it also often had a magical significance, and clansmen sometimes thought it protected its wearer from evil.

Fraser – wild strawberry

Wallace – pine

MacDonald – heather

Badges and mottos

The chief's badge and motto usually recall a famous episode from the history of the clan. Here are a few clan badges and mottos. You might try making one for yourself. Several more are shown on page 3.

Ne obliviscaris – Do not forget! – (Campbell)
Bydand – Enduring – (Gordon)
Veritas vincit – Truth overcomes – (Keith)
Per mare per terras – By sea and land – (MacDonald)
'S rioghal mo dhream – My race is royal – (MacGregor)
Manu forti – With a strong hand – (Mackay)
Pro libertate – For liberty! – (Wallace)

The use of charms and amulets in the Highlands points to a strong belief in the supernatural powers present in the dramatic landscape. Traditional 'folk-medicine' was also practised, using local plants and herbs.

More formal religion has always been an important part of the Highland way of life. Since the Irish missionary Columba and his followers brought Christianity to the Highlands and Islands from Iona in the 6th century, the evidence of his work can still be seen today. There are many church dedications to the saint and the influence of the Celtic Church is still very strong.

Campbell

From the 12th to 16th centuries, the Church in the Highlands was Catholic, but the Scottish Reformation of 1560 brought about great change. Religion in most of the Highlands, using the Gaelic language and adopting its own unique traditions, became strongly Presbyterian. Today many faiths are practised in the region. Its landscape provides inspiration for all.

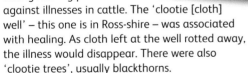

Amber beads (above) were thought to have protective powers to cure eye disease, while rock crystal (right) held strong healing powers against illnesses in cattle. The 'clootie [cloth] well' – this one is in Ross-shire – was associated with healing. As cloth left at the well rotted away, the illness would disappear. There were also 'clootie trees', usually blackthorns.

Wearing badges

A similar idea to the clan identity can be seen in the wearing of school uniforms or football scarves and colours. Perhaps you have noticed such badges or symbols as Welsh people wearing a daffodil on St David's Day; or Irish people wearing a shamrock on St Patrick's day; or members of the Labour Party wearing a red rose

What is the idea behind wearing a poppy, for example, and when do we wear one? In England, there is the Red Rose county and the White Rose county. What is the significance of the rose to these counties?

Answers on page 40

Clan gatherings and games

Clan gatherings grew out of summer meetings, held by the clan chiefs to discuss matters of importance.

Competitions were also held at these meetings, so that young clansmen could test their strength and fitness. Chiefs could select their personal bodyguards from the strongest clansmen, and the fastest runners would become their messengers. The clan's safety and security depended on the strength of its warriors and the speed of its runners.

Clansmen showed their strength by wrestling, weightlifting and throwing, and tug-of-war. Their agility was tested by running, sprinting, jumping and vaulting. The hill race was one of the most difficult tests. According to an old story, King Malcolm Canmore organised one of these events above Braemar during the 11th century.

Today's gatherings

Today's Highland games are our modern version of the old clan games. Each summer, about sixty events take place all over Scotland. A chief is usually appointed to organise modern games, as in earlier times, and as well as sporting events, there is usually piping and dancing competitions.

Above: A souvenir programme of the Highland Games held in Cobourg, Ontario, Canada, in 1966. Below this is a poster advertising the 'Gathering of the Clans' in Pugwash, Nova Scotia, in 1979.

38

Nowadays these Scottish gatherings are also held all over the world, especially in the USA and Canada. Thousands of clansmen emigrated to North America during the Clearances of the 18th and 19th century as well as later (see page 27).

Today, more than 20 million North Americans claim Scottish descent, and many people in Nova Scotia, Canada, speak Gaelic. Many Americans nowadays are deeply interested in their roots and family history. So the spirit of kinship and shared heritage is probably as strong at these modern events – especially the overseas ones – as it was in past times.

(see page 27)

What's in a name?

Find out about your own genealogy and family tree using ScotlandsPeople* at:

www.scotlandspeople.gov.uk

The site provides access to the statutory registers of births, marriages and deaths; census returns; church records; valuation rolls; and legal records from Scotland's courts of law. You can use it to research family, local and social history

*Run by a partnership between the National Records of Scotland and the Court of the Lord Lyon

Far left: Emigrants from the Isle of Lewis, working as lumberjacks in the Canadian forest in 1905.

Left: Pipers, young and old, bid farewell to Scots setting out for a new life abroad.

Below: The Highland sport of shinty was taken all over the world by migrating Scots. In Canada it was played on frozen lakes during winter, evolving into the national sport of ice hockey.

Scotland and the World

The place name **Nova Scotia** is Latin for **New Scotland**. Have a look at a map of the east coast of Canada. What do the placenames tell us about the people who live there?

Find out about Nova Scotia. Use an atlas or gazetteer to find other Scottish placenames elsewhere in the world. Apart from Scotland and Canada, where are most of them to be found?

Answers on page 40

Answers on page 40

ANSWERS

Page 7: **Private army** – The Dukes of Atholl keep the only private army left in Britain, at Blair Castle, Perthshire. They are chiefs of the clan Murray.

Page 9: **Mystery object** – This shield or targe was held by a strap over the arm. Highlanders in the 17th century added brass or silver nails to the front of it. The leather surface was often tooled with animals or leafy scrolls. The double eagle on this targe is the heraldic badge of the MacDonalds, Lords of the Isles.

Page 13: **Gaelic placename meanings** – Ballochbuie = yellow pass; Inverness = mouth of river Ness; Dundonald = Donald's castle; Braemar = upland of Mar; Kyles of Bute = narrow straits of Bute; Strathspey = broad valley of the Spey; Ben More = big mountain; Inchkenneth = Kenneth's island; Kilpatrick = Patrick's church; Kilcreggan = church on the little rock; Tobermory = Mary's well; Kinloch-leven = head of Loch Leven

Page 19: **Mystery object** – This object comes from a Highland bagpipe chanter. It is a view looking up the mouth of the chanter – the bit at the very bottom. **Paying the piper!** – If you are paying the piper's wages, it is up to you to tell him what tunes to play!

Page 22: **Biggest cannon** – The biggest cannon in King James II's artillery was called 'Mons Meg', a gift from the Duke of Burgundy to the King of Scots in 1457. Today Mons Meg is at Edinburgh Castle.

Page 25: **Clans versus king** – The main reason why the clans never united against the king was that they were too busy fighting each other.

Page 32: **Mystery object** – A stick bound with wool samples coloured with dye of native Scottish plants. Sample 5 is bracken, 6 is heather, and 7 and 8 come from onion skins. Samples 9 and 10 are exceptions: They were dyed with indigo which became available through foreign trade in the late middle ages.

Page 37: **The poppy** is worn on Armistice Day (11 November) to remember the fallen of two World Wars. The poppy as a symbol comes from the fields of poppies in Flanders, the scene of terrible carnage during the First World War. **The rose** gave its name to the English Wars of the Roses during the 15th century, when the succession to the English throne was fought over by rival families. Lancashire was the Red Rose county and Yorkshire the White.

Page 39: **Scotland and the World** – Scottish place names in eastern Canada include Campbelltown, Dalhousie, Port Elgin and Inverness. There are also English names such as Halifax, Dartmouth and Newcastle; French names (Cape Breton, Port aux Basques, Mount Joli), and First Nation names (Miramichi Bay, Natashquan, Chicoutimi). Other countries with Scottish names include South Africa (Fraserburg, Aberdeen), Australia (Perth, Cairns, Mackay), New Zealand (Invercargill, Hamilton and Dunedin).

USEFUL WEBSITES

National Museums Scotland
    www.nms.ac.uk

National Trust for Scotland
    www.nts.org.uk

Piping   www.musicplockton.org
    (The National Centre of Excellence in Traditional Music at Plockton High School)
    rspba.org
    (Royal Scottish Pipe Band Association, Glasgow)

Regimental history
    www.theblackwatch.co.uk
    www.argylls.co.uk
    www.theroyalscots.co.uk

Tartans
    www.tartanregister.gov.uk

Visit Scotland
    https://www.visitscotland.com/see-do/research-your-ancestry/clans/

Wikipedia
    www.wikipedia.org

ANSWERS

Facts and activities section –

Page iv: **Word search** – The 18 words related to the Gaelic language or to the Highlands are highlighted in the box below.

Page v: **Criss-crossword** – (1) Gaelic; (2) quaich; (3) Culloden; (4) patronymic; (5) clarsach; (6) bagpipes; (7) Walter Scott; (8) sporran; (9) amulet

K	I	N	L	O	C	H	L	E	V	E	N	C	J
B	S	A	H	G	R	A	E	F	D	R	C	A	T
U	A	Z	T	L	N	Q	O	I	J	G	T	O	B
X	O	L	L	G	S	N	M	V	W	L	B	L	B
H	F	A	L	Q	L	R	I	D	C	E	G	G	I
H	E	S	G	Q	A	E	I	E	R	N	Q	R	X
C	C	I	U	I	C	E	A	M	B	E	R	A	J
B	R	A	D	D	D	H	O	N	D	A	S	B	R
C	W	L	L	R	L	R	B	U	N	G	T	O	Y
I	E	G	E	A	Y	O	N	U	X	L	R	T	E
Q	B	A	R	R	E	P	C	A	I	E	A	F	Z
L	X	E	M	P	N	B	I	H	P	S	T	I	J
P	K	C	U	B	R	A	I	G	H	E	H	L	S
G	A	R	O	M	B	M	Y	Y	O	T	A	D	Y

The Clans
Facts and activities

This book belongs to:

_____

Write your name on the above line.

Design a clan badge

Clan badges traditionally included a motto that recalled an episode from the history of the clan. The motto can be inspiring or something to frighten your enemies!

Tartan weave

Tartan continues to be worn and celebrated all over the world, especially in the fashion houses of New York, London and Paris. But how is this famous fabric woven?

Making a tartan **sett** (or pattern) may appear quite complicated, but it's actually quite simple.

1. First, a regular sequence of coloured stripes of varying widths are woven.

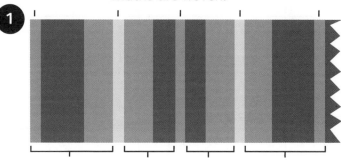

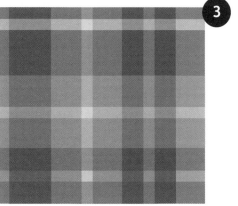

2. The sequence is then reversed, then repeated, then reversed, and so on.

3. The same sequence is then interwoven at right angles to the first sequence. The two sequences are called the **warp** (vertical) and the **weft** (horizontal).

Word search

Move diagonally, as well as up and down,
in any direction, to discover the 18 Gaelic or
Highland words and names listed below.

Answers on page 40

K	I	N	L	O	C	H	L	E	V	E	N	C	J
B	S	A	H	G	R	A	E	F	D	R	C	A	T
U	A	Z	T	L	N	Q	O	I	J	G	T	O	B
X	O	L	L	G	S	N	M	V	W	L	B	L	B
H	F	A	L	Q	L	R	I	D	C	E	G	G	I
H	E	S	G	O	A	E	E	R	N	Q	R	X
C	C	I	U	I	C	I	A	M	B	E	R	A	J
B	R	A	D	D	D	H	O	N	D	A	S	B	R
C	W	L	L	R	L	R	B	U	N	G	T	O	Y
I	E	G	E	A	Y	O	N	U	X	L	R	T	E
Q	B	A	R	R	E	P	C	A	I	E	A	F	Z
L	X	E	M	P	N	B	I	H	P	S	T	I	J
P	K	C	U	B	R	A	I	G	H	E	H	L	S
G	A	R	O	M	B	M	Y	Y	O	T	A	D	Y

BARR	CEALL	GLEANN	STRATH
BEALACH	DIARMID	GLENEAGLES	TOBAR
BEINN	DUN	KINLOCHLEVEN	TOBERMORY
BRAIGHE	EAGLAIS	LOCH	
CAOL	FEARGHAS	MORAG	

Criss-crossword

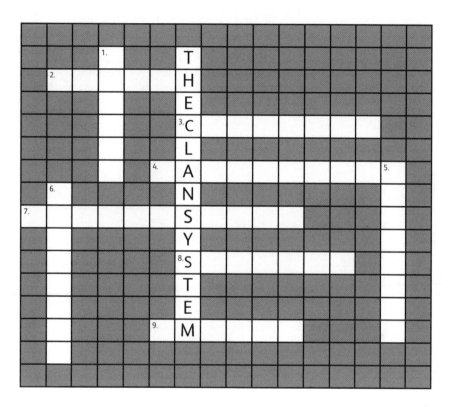

Answer the following questions to complete this word puzzle. There is a phrase completed already to start you off:

1. The language of the Highland clans. (See pages 12-13)
2. A traditional Highland drinking cup. (See page 20)
3. A famous battle in April 1746. (See page 27)
4. A type of surname that is based on the father's name. (See pages 10-11)
5. The Gaelic word for a harp. (See page 18)
6. An instrument that is mostly connected with Scotland. (See pages 18-19)
7. The well-known Scottish writer with an apt Scottish name. (See pages 28-29)
8. Instead of pockets on a kilt. (See page 31)
9. A charm worn to ward off evil and disease (See page 37)

Answers on page 40

The drover's road

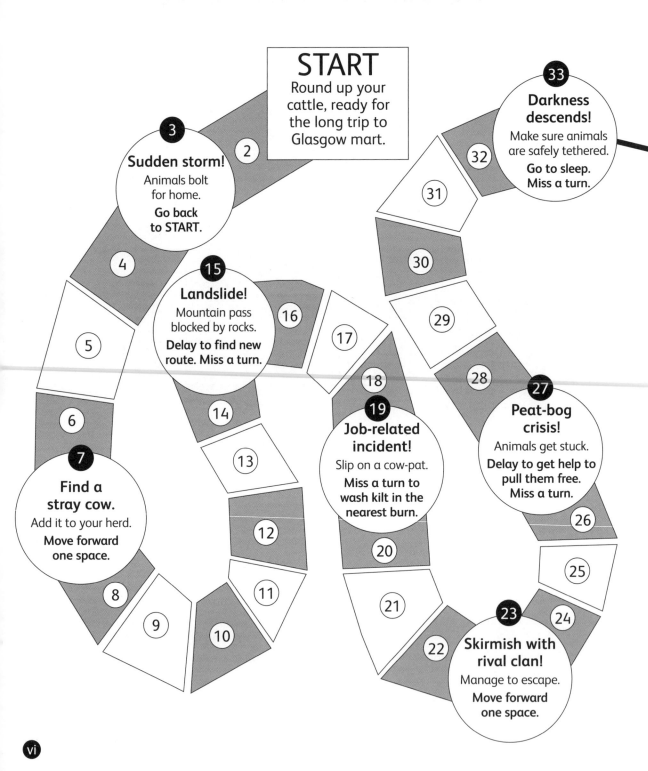

START
Round up your cattle, ready for the long trip to Glasgow mart.

3 **Sudden storm!**
Animals bolt for home.
Go back to START.

2

4

5

6

7 **Find a stray cow.**
Add it to your herd.
Move forward one space.

8

9

10

11

12

13

14

15 **Landslide!**
Mountain pass blocked by rocks.
Delay to find new route. Miss a turn.

16

17

18

19 **Job-related incident!**
Slip on a cow-pat.
Miss a turn to wash kilt in the nearest burn.

20

21

22

23 **Skirmish with rival clan!**
Manage to escape.
Move forward one space.

24

25

26

27 **Peat-bog crisis!**
Animals get stuck.
Delay to get help to pull them free. Miss a turn.

28

29

30

31

32

33 **Darkness descends!**
Make sure animals are safely tethered.
Go to sleep. Miss a turn.

This is a game for 2 to 4 players. You will need a dice and a small counter for each player. Follow the instructions on the spaces you land on.

To move, throw the dice. The winner is the player who reaches the Glasgow Mart first!

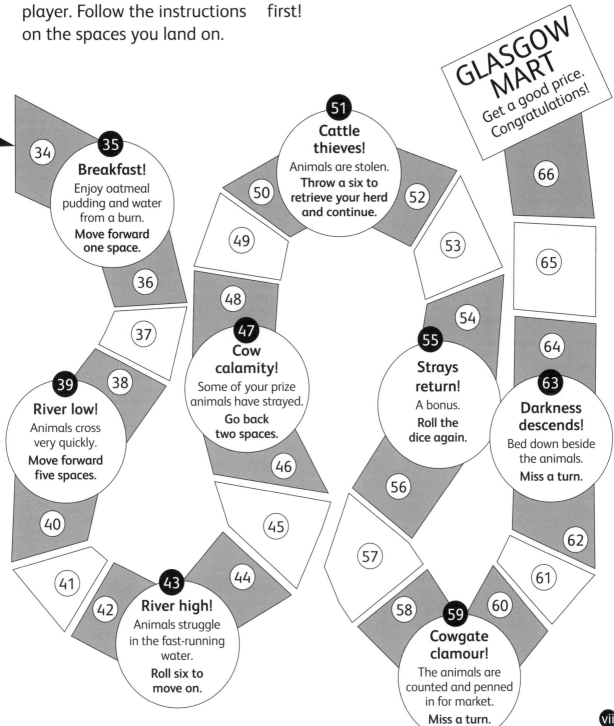

GLASGOW MART
Get a good price.
Congratulations!

34

35
Breakfast!
Enjoy oatmeal pudding and water from a burn.
Move forward one space.

36

37

38

39
River low!
Animals cross very quickly.
Move forward five spaces.

40

41

42

43
River high!
Animals struggle in the fast-running water.
Roll six to move on.

44

45

46

47
Cow calamity!
Some of your prize animals have strayed.
Go back two spaces.

48

49

50

51
Cattle thieves!
Animals are stolen.
Throw a six to retrieve your herd and continue.

52

53

54

55
Strays return!
A bonus.
Roll the dice again.

56

57

58

59
Cowgate clamour!
The animals are counted and penned in for market.
Miss a turn.

60

61

62

63
Darkness descends!
Bed down beside the animals.
Miss a turn.

64

65

66

PLACES OF INTEREST

Listed below are a number of places associated with Clan activities and histories in Scotland:

Argyll and Sutherland Highlanders' Museum, Stirling Castle

The Black Watch Museum, Balhousie Castle, Hay Street, Perth

Blair Castle, Blair Atholl, Perthshire [clan: Murray]

Brodie Castle, near Forres, Moray

Castle Menzies, Weem, by Aberfeldy, Perthshire

Clan Cameron Museum, Achnacarry, Spean Bridge, Inverness-shire

Museum of the Isles, Armadale, Sleat, Isle of Skye

Clan Donnachaidh Museum, Bruar Falls, Blair Atholl, Perthshire [clan: Robertson]

Clan Gunn Heritage Centre, Latheron, Caithness

Clan Macpherson Museum, Newtonmore, Inverness-shire

Clan Ross Centre, Tain, Ross & Cromarty

Duart Castle, Craignure, Isle of Mull [clan: MacLean of Duart]

Dunvegan Castle, Isle of Skye [clan: MacLeod] [clan: Kerr]

Glencoe and North Lorn Folk Museum, Glencoe Village, Argyll

Gordon Highlanders Museum, Aberdeen

Highland Folk Museum, Kingussie, Inverness-shire

Inveraray Castle, Inveraray, Argyll [clan: Campbell]

Inverness Museum, Inverness

National Museums Scotland including the **National Museum of Scotland**, Chambers Street, Edinburgh; and **National War Museum of Scotland** at Edinburgh Castle

The National Piping Centre, Glasgow

The Highlanders Museum, Fort George, Inverness-shire

Strathnaver Museum, near Bettyhill, Sutherland [clan: Mackay; also the Clearances]

Weavers' Cottages, Kilbarchan, Renfrewshire

West Highland Museum, Fort William, Lochaber

FURTHER CREDITS

OTHER TITLES IN THE NEW SCOTTIES SERIES (edited by Frances and Gordon Jarvie)